4.7

W9-AXA-167

pts

Quiz # 26828

RELIGIONS OF THE WORLD

I Am
Baptist

❋ PATRICIA HARRINGTON ❋

The Rosen Publishing Group's
PowerKids Press™
New York

Published in 1999 by The Rosen Publishing Group, Inc.
29 East 21st Street, New York, NY 10010

First Edition

Book Design: Erin McKenna and Kim Sonsky

Photo Credits: p. 4 © Arthur Tilley/FPG International; p. 8 © Art Resource; p. 11 © Erich Lessing/Art Resource; p. 12 © UPI/Corbis-Bettmann; p.15 © Chuck Mason/International Stock; pp. 16, 19, 20 © Jeff Greenberg/Archive Photos.

Harrington, Patricia, 1969–
    I am Baptist / by Patricia Harrington.
        p.   cm. — (Religions of the world)
    Summary: A young Baptist girl introduces the history, beliefs, and practices
of this Christian religion.
    ISBN 0-8239-5261-4
    1. Baptists—Juvenile literature. [1. Baptists.] I. Title. II. Series: Religions of the world
(Rosen Publishing Group)
BX6331.2.H25 1998
286—dc21   98-20143
                                                         CIP
                                                            AC

Manufactured in the United States of America

Contents

Valerie

Hi! I'm Valerie, and I'm Baptist. The Baptist **faith** (FAYTH) is part of the Christian religion. All Christians follow the teachings of a man named Jesus Christ. But not all Christians believe in the exact same things. Most Christians are either Catholic or Protestant. **Protestantism** (PRAH-tuh-stant-izm) is made up of people who believe in lots of different faiths, such as Lutherans, Presbyterians, and Methodists. Baptists are also Protestant.

◀ There are millions of Baptists all over the world. You may even have a friend who's a Baptist.

Baptist Beginnings

In the seventeenth century, people in England were expected to follow the religious beliefs of King James I. Some people left the country to find the freedom to practice whatever religion they wanted. One of those people was a man named John Smyth. He went to Holland in search of religious freedom. Smyth met some other English people there who shared his beliefs. In 1609, they started the first Baptist church together.

In order to practice the religion they wanted, English people like ▶
John Smyth had to travel to other countries like Holland.

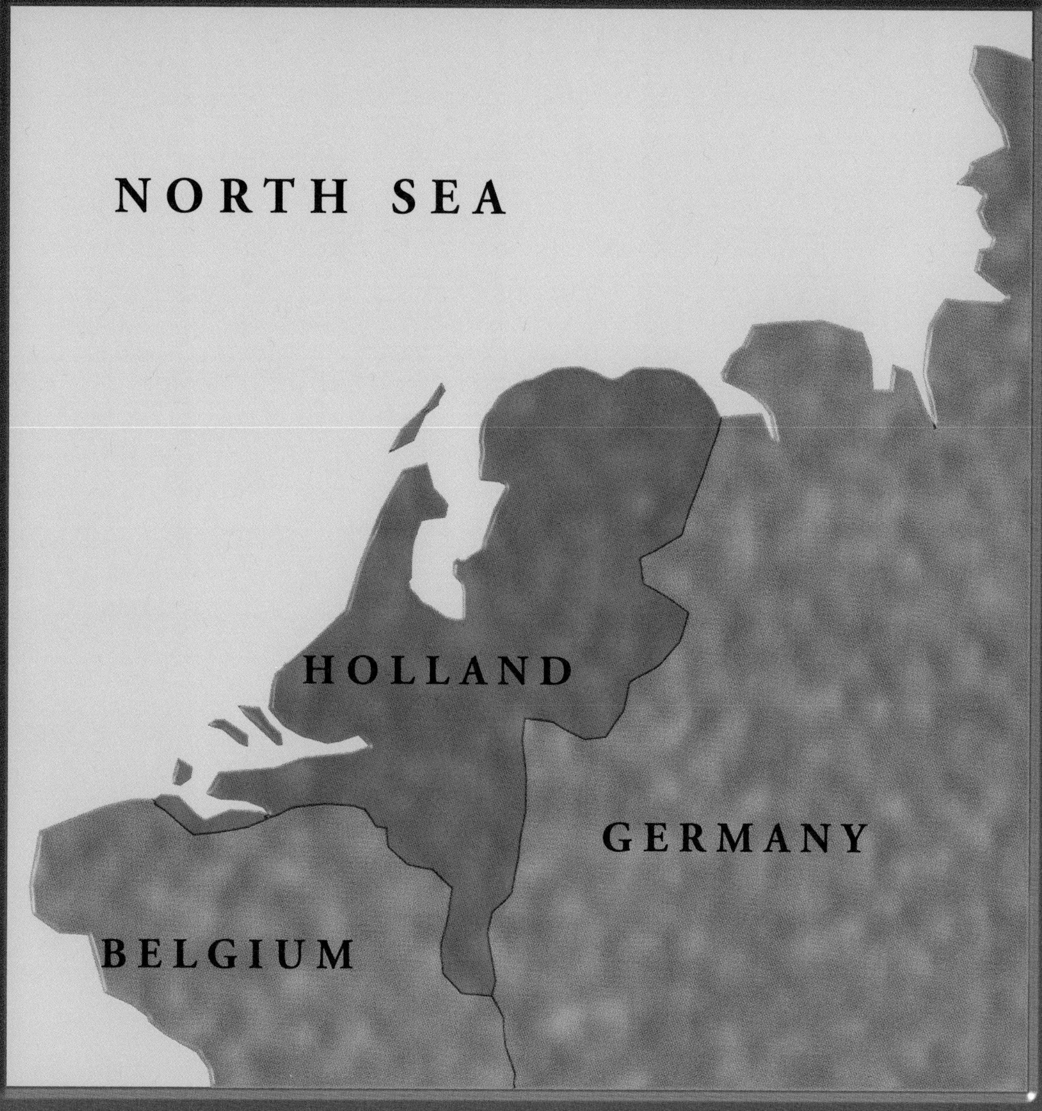
NORTH SEA
HOLLAND
GERMANY
BELGIUM

Freedom of Religion

Smyth and the other people who became Baptists left England because the English **monarchy** (MON-ar-kee) was telling people what they should think and how they should live their lives. They wanted the chance to follow their own **beliefs** (buh-LEEFS). So for Baptists today, it's very important that religion and government are separate. Baptists believe that everyone should have the right to choose his or her own faith.

◄ The monarchy controlled the country from large castles such as this one in Trent, England.

Baptists in Early America

Many English people traveled to Holland and other European countries seeking religious freedom. Still others went to America. But while these early Americans wanted to practice their beliefs in their own way, they didn't always want others to do the same. When Baptists came to America soon afterward, they had a hard time practicing their religion in peace. But they didn't let that stop them.

Wherever they were, Baptists continued to follow what they believed. This included practicing ▶ church services in their own way.

How Baptists Got Their Name

Many Christians are baptized, including Baptists. In some churches, people are quickly **submerged** (sub-MERJD), which means they are placed under water. This is called **immersion** (im-ER-zhun). In other churches, they are just sprinkled with water.

In baptism, the use of water represents getting rid of old ways and starting over. Some Christians baptize babies, but Baptists don't. They believe people should be old enough to decide when they're ready to be baptized.

◀ Family and church members all take part in a Baptist baptism.

Can You Be Born Again?

One important part of the Baptist religion is being reborn. Christians believe that when people are born, they aren't as good as they could be. But if they believe in God, and are sorry for all their **sins** (SINZ), they can be "reborn," or "born again." When a Christian is reborn it means that she is going to try to be the kind of person she thinks God wants her to be. A Christian becomes reborn through **baptism** (BAP-tiz-um).

Prayer is one way that Baptists keep themselves closer to God and away from sin. ▶

God's Words

The Bible was written by many people. But Baptists believe that the words in the Bible are actually God's words. Baptists think God gave His words to special people who then recorded them for Him in the Bible. Because of this, Baptists consider the Bible to be their guide on how to live. For example, Baptists believe the Christians in the Bible were baptized by immersion. That's why many Baptists are baptized this way today.

◀ Baptists learn about the Bible the first time they go to church. It is a very important part of the Baptist faith.

One Faith, Different Styles

There are many different kinds of Baptists. Southern Baptists are often **evangelical** (ee-van-JEL-ih-kul). This means they follow their lives strictly by the words of the Bible. Most Baptists go to church, but there are different kinds of Baptist church services. In some churches, Baptists listen to a **pastor** (PAS-ter) speak about the Bible and then listen to a **choir** (QUI-er) sing **hymns** (HIMZ). In other churches, people talk to their pastor as he speaks, and sing along with the hymns.

At all kinds of Baptist churches everyone takes part in the service. ▶

Missionaries

Although Baptists believe that people have the right to choose their religion, they also want everyone to know about the Baptist faith. Baptist **missionaries** (MIH-shun-ayr-eez) teach people about their religion. When someone decides to become a Baptist, it's called a **conversion** (kun-VER-zhun). People who go through a conversion are called converts. Baptist missionaries have been very successful. There are Baptist converts in countries all over the world.

◀ Converts are always welcomed into the Baptist church by the church minister and its other members.

A Shared Faith

Before John Smyth and his English friends started their new church, they weren't able to practice their religion in their own homes because of the English monarchy. When Baptists came to America, they had the same trouble. However, almost four hundred years later, there are millions of Baptists in the United States and around the world. In fact, it's one of the largest Protestant faiths. Whenever a person is baptized into the Baptist faith, he or she is sharing beliefs and **traditions** (truh-DIH-shunz) with Baptists all over the world.

Glossary

baptism (BAP-tiz-um) The religious practice of symbolically washing away sins with water.

belief (buh-LEEF) Something that is thought to be believed.

choir (QUI-er) A group of people who sing at a religious service.

conversion (kun-VER-zhun) The way in which a person becomes part of a new religion.

evangelical (ee-van-JEL-ih-kul) Relating to something which is strongly based on a life guided by the Bible.

faith (FAYTH) A belief and trust in God.

hymn (HIM) A song that honors God.

immersion (im-ER-zhun) Baptism by briefly submerging someone in water.

missionary (MIH-shun-ayr-ee) A person who teaches his religion to people with different beliefs.

monarchy (MON-ar-kee) A government run by a king or queen.

pastor (PAS-ter) A minister in charge of a church.

Protestantism (PRAH-tuh-stant-izm) A religion based on Christian beliefs which includes many smaller groups.

sin (SIN) A wrongdoing.

submerge (sub-MERJ) To cover with water.

tradition (truh-DIH-shun) Something a group of people has done the same way for a long time.

Index